WHY ONLY TWO SLICES OF THE BREAD?

CHANGING HOW YOU APPROACH LIFE

O'NEIL B. ANKLE AND
WAZER H. WALKER

author HOUSE®

AuthorHouse™
1663 Liberty Drive
Bloomington, IN 47403
www.authorhouse.com
Phone: 833-262-8899

Published by AuthorHouse 06/24/2021

ISBN: 978-1-6655-2777-4 (sc)
ISBN: 978-1-6655-2776-7 (hc)
ISBN: 978-1-6655-2775-0 (e)

Library of Congress Control Number: 2021911108

This book was edited by

Helloise Louden, former head of the Department of English at Knox College, Spaulding, Clarendon, Jamaica

Cheryl Brown-Harper, senior English Educator at Jonathan Grant High School, Spanish Town, St. Catherine, Jamaica

Bible Scriptures are taken from the King James Version of the Bible. Public Domain.

Scripture taken from the New King James Version®. Copyright © 1982 by Thomas Nelson. Used by permission. All rights reserved.

Contents

DEDICATION

To our wives, Marcia Ankle and Karen Walker,

and our children: OJ, Rochelle, Joel, Ruth-

Ann, and Winnifred (O'Neil's mom)

But be ye doers of the word, and not hearers

only, deceiving your own selves.

(James 1:22)

Introduction

Without a shadow of a doubt, we have been placed on the earth at a time such as this, where many people feel dejected, depressed, and overwhelmed by the circumstances they face in their lives. This feeling applies to all ages. Our calling is to help people in whatever shape or form to overcome many of the obstacles they are likely to face, and that may derail them off the path of success.

It is hoped that the words of this book will encourage and motivate you. It's our wish that reading this book will also cause you to be more closely drawn to Jesus Christ, our Hope, Savior, and Lord.

We also hope that parents and students will find this book an inspiration and will help strengthen their beliefs that they are God's chosen vessels. With the Covid-19 pandemic raging across the world, people need to have hope and faith in Jesus Christ alone.

There is a great deal of negativity in the world; hence, the text is aimed at helping to drive you into purpose and the will of God. There is no reason why people should wake up each day and be fed with a steady diet of negative energy. Paul, speaking to the Philippians in chapter 4 verse 8, said, "Finally, brethren, whatsoever things are true, whatsoever, things are honest, whatsoever things are just, whatsoever things are pure, whatsoever things are lovely, whatsoever things are of good report; if there be any virtue, and if there be any praise, think on these things." Essentially, what you consume in your minds is manifested into action. It's important to keep a filter over your mind and thoughts, so that honest, pure, and righteous things emanate from you.

Replace harmful thoughts with God's word daily. Can it be done? Yes! Commit yourself, and it will work. It will take time, but it starts with a commitment.

CHAPTER 1

Two Slices of the Bread

Reality is built out of thought, and our every thought

begins to create reality. – Edgar Cayce

There is an understanding that our thoughts can allow us to accomplish many things. "Death and life are in the power of the tongue: and they that love it shall eat the fruit thereof" (Proverbs 18:21).

It therefore means that if you downsize your thinking process and put things in a little box, the outcome is likely to be tiny and insignificant. Furthermore, to pint-size your thoughts, beliefs, and dreams is exactly what you are likely to achieve. Pint-sized dreams will bring blessings of similar measure.

It is through your thought processes that you may determine your accomplishments. Why not adopt the principle of big thinking, or dreaming big, or above and beyond blessings? Why limit your capacity to achieve, when you were created for achieving excellence, success, and victory and having more than enough? You were created to soar even when you may be working against the wind of adversity. "And the LORD shall make you the head, not the tail; and thou shalt be above only, and thou shalt not be beneath" (Deuteronomy 28:13).

The process of becoming the head starts within one's mind. Despite working with the concept that says, "If I launch out, something positive can happen," achievements will not come without struggles. Someone holding you back along with stagnation may have been your lot. However, it does not have to be a death sentence. You are better than that. Learn to talk to *you*.

The struggle you will face on your way to progress will make you stronger. You will therefore come out of your struggle smiling, knowing that it was worth it. Purpose is never achieved without some kind of setback or failure. Nothing in this life worth having will come without some struggle.

Your Struggle Can Give You Strength

It has been said that in the metamorphosis of a caterpillar into a butterfly, if the natural process is disturbed, the struggle will not be the same. When the wings appear from the cocoon, if you pull them in an effort to assist the emerging butterfly, it doesn't matter how beautiful it looks, it will never fly. This is so, because it is the pushing, the struggle against the cocoon over time that will strengthen the wings of the insect and allow it to fly when it emerges from that ugly case. So in life, we go through challenges and struggles, some greater than others. Depending on how you view and approach these impediments, they will either make you strong enough to fly like the butterfly or ground you for life. And then you blame everyone else except yourself.

Why limit your thinking and marginalize your dreams? Why set a twelve-ounce bucket to catch water when you actually need a hundred-gallon drum to last you? Part of the challenge most of us have is that we limit what we can accomplish because we place restrictions and limitations on our thoughts, visions, and missions to think big. In so doing, we also limit God and what He can do for us. Why then limit the extent of your faith and settle for less than the best?

To achieve anything in this life, you should not settle with only two slices of the bread when you can have the complete loaf. Better yet, why become comfortable with the loaf, when you can have the bakery or the field where the wheat is grown? Go for all that constitutes running the bakery. Essentially, look at the bigger picture of what you can achieve. Frame your thoughts around elevating who you are. The gutter was never made for you—it was constructed for debris and water. I hope you have got the picture in your mind.

I challenge you to move out of your comfort zone and begin to go for the bakery as you set out your plans to accomplish great things. Go for your dreams. It is big dreamers and thinkers who are going to grasp opportunities with both hands when they present themselves. Stop at nothing, as long as it is morally and ethically correct, in the accomplishment of your desires. God did not create you to place limits on yourself or your gifts.

Because of our circumstances, situations, where we were born, who raised us, and the negative diet that we were steadily fed daily, we place limitations on our lives, our aspirations, and our dreams.

If you can own the property where the corn or wheat is grown to make the bread, why then settle for the bakery or only two slices of the bread? Get greedy in a positive sense. Stop fishing in the shallow water, and launch out into the deep. In other words, if your dream is to go into business, do not downsize the vision.

Simply put, if the transportation sector is your dream, why settle with just one taxi and live from hand to mouth? What if you dream of owning three or four taxis, or for that matter envision establishing a fleet and dispatch centers in the same breath? What about a chain of internet cafés instead of one? What about owning a fleet of trucks to transport goods? Instead of one salon, dream of several across the major towns and cities. What about buying into one of those major food franchises?

This kind of thinking is not limited to those who have godfathers or godmothers, or those living in particular communities. While it may be a factor, it cannot be the only one. You have to trust and believe in yourself. Invest in your dreams while you are doing same. Subsequently, one should purpose in one's heart never to be satisfied with only two slices of the bread.

Unwind out of that cocoon. It's time to remove the shackles of limitation from your minds and go chase your dreams.

This year, I challenge you to become a purpose-driven chaser. Look at all the obstacles and criticisms as stepping-stones and power builders.

If striving for more than two slices of the bread connotes going beyond the regular to achieve the desired goals, you should not settle for two. If there is an A on the table, why not go for it? Stop being mediocre by settling for a grade C. Far too many of us are comfortable with being average and ordinary. It's time to switch to the realm of the extraordinary. Track and field world beaters like Shelly-Ann Frazer Pryce, Usain Bolt, Veronica Campbell-Brown, and cricketer Chris Gayle could not have been ordinary and still performed on the world stage of sports as they did. Understandably, to evolve from being ordinary to being extraordinary will take a lot of hard work, sacrifice, and dedication.

You cannot be ordinary when you were created from one out of a possible million or more sperm cells. You did not survive such odds to be ordinary. It was a very competitive but serious swim to that egg (ovum) for an attachment, and guess what? You won! Hence you are not ordinary or regular but premium. You are specially and uniquely designed by God to rise to the top like the crème de la crème. Think and act like it. No human can dream for another. The individual can only help to shape the dream and make it manifest itself. Someone else—a mentor, perhaps—may become conscious of how great and awesome you can be, yet you have to be the one to make the vision or the dream clear.

Write Your Vison

Seek always to write your vision; it is biblical. Habakkuk 2:2 intimates, "Write the vision, and make it plain upon tables, that he may run that readeth it."

Each of us ought to dream and have a vision of where we want success to take us. Success starts in the mind. But how do you envision it?

Many who have made it in this life have been dreaming and wanting to do better than their parents. They didn't get comfortable with only two slices of the bread. They wanted more. These persons never allowed their environment or circumstances of birth to be their millstone. They were willing to get out of the box where they were placed, many times by society, friends, communities, and even family members.

Most great individuals of this world did not become great by simply thinking about it.

> Most great individuals of this world did not become great by simply thinking about it. They acted!

They acted! Dream, but act; think big, and act on it. Allow your thought processes to take you into unknown territories. But you must take action and broaden your horizons. Never sit around waiting for a golden egg to fall from the sky into your lap. Such a wait will be eternal.

While the journey of achieving your set goals and desires may be a stretch, one must be patient and endeavor not to be absorbed by the microwave culture, wanting everything even faster than how that appliance can warm up a Cup-a-Soup.

Question: Do you have a vision board? Have you written down all you want to achieve over the next thirty-six months? This may number over two hundred items, but don't worry. It's important that the vision board becomes a part of the journey, since the goal is elevating your life. As you go along, eliminate what you have achieved. In the end you will surprise yourself. Oops! There is no age limitation to this strategy. There is no expiration date to your vision or dream.

*If you correct your mind, the rest of your
life will fall into place.* – Lao Tzu

I am master of my fate and captain of

my destiny. – Nelson Mandela

Trust in the LORD with all thine heart; and lean not unto thine own understanding. In all thy ways acknowledge him, and he shall direct thy path. (Proverbs 3:5–6)

Prayer

Holy Father, You who are Omnipotent, Omniscient, and Omnipresent: in the name of Jesus Christ, I ask that You show me how to reach for the stars and how not to limit my potential, dreams, and ambitions. Amen.

CHAPTER 2

Are you pregnant? If so, with what?

Giving birth and being born brings us into the essence of creation, where the human spirit is courageous and bold and the body, a miracle of wisdom. – Harriette Hartigan

Some years ago, while I was addressing a group of boys at a prominent high school in the central region of Jamaica, they were told that I was pregnant. You guessed it right, they laughed uncontrollably. That was, of course natural, and I expected it. However, when I explained to them why I was pregnant, that's when they composed themselves. Figuratively speaking, I believe that all of us, male and female alike, are pregnant. There are some of us who are able to carry this pregnancy and give birth, while there are those who may decide to abort theirs. Whom you choose to run and rub shoulders with may well determine whether or not you give birth.

To be metaphorically pregnant is to have an expectancy of something. Ask any woman who is pregnant, especially for the first time, about the joy that comes with it and the expected arrival of that child or children. Almost any woman who is pregnant with a child expects a healthy baby, she hopes it will bring her joy and happiness to her partner.

From observation, when a woman is pregnant, there is constant preparation during the pregnancy and bated anticipation for the expected child. In life, the woman has to visit her general practitioner or a specialist to make sure that all is well with the pregnancy. The woman also has to go shopping to procure baby necessities. The mother-to-be wants to know that she is more than prepared for the arrival of this child. Sometimes the expectant mother is even overprepared for the birth. But it is better to be overprepared than to be underprepared.

So, as it is with a literal pregnancy in terms of preparation, the same is true for the figurative pregnancy to which I refer. When I told the boys I was pregnant, I expected a resounding no!! However, no matter how old you are, you can become pregnant without being sexually involved. To be pregnant metaphorically is to be pregnant with

- Purpose
- Success
- Excellence
- Dreams and Aspirations
- Desires
- Achievements

For each one of those listed, you have to give birth to it. If you are on the road to success, it is important that you give birth to it and the process must not be aborted. Giving birth to your successes, dreams, and aspirations will require you to find mentors and the right people to run and walk with. You must be careful of whom you have in your corner. No matter what, a boxer is always expected to have positive persons in his or her corner. Success is always built on encouragement and motivation. There is nothing wrong with shedding some persons from your life circle. When you go into orbit, not all the rockets can travel with you.

If you should fall on your way to your dreams and aspirations— and there are likely to be potholes and ditches along the way—don't give in. The old adage is if you can look up, you can get up. So if you slip along the way, get up, shake yourself off, and start again.

Failure Is Never Permanent

Failure is never permanent; it's just a delay to your success and greatness. You fail when you remain down, wallowing in the gutter of self-pity or allowing people's mouth to keep you in a state of mental flux and trepidation. Read the history of Abraham Lincoln, the sixteenth president of the United States, and you will find that he suffered many setbacks in his life before becoming president. Founder and former CEO of Microsoft Bill Gates failed at business before rising in the world of technology. Today he is worth billions. His name is also synonymous with the world of computers.

What about J. K. Rowling, the author of the Harry Potter series? Before her golden success, she was unemployed and on welfare, a divorced mother who was going to school and trying to write a book in her spare time. Before his success, recording artist and producer Jay-Z (Shawn Corey Carter) was rejected by several major recording companies. He did not give up on his dreams. The Brooklyn native reacted by starting his own recording company. His net worth today is literally off the charts. Do you see yourself in some of these notables? Can you see yourself leapfrogging into success?

Never make failure your destination as it can be mentally paralyzing and

Never make failure your destination, as it can be mentally paralyzing and debilitating.

debilitating. There are so many stories of success out there. Following failure, great basketballer Michael Jordan, Oprah

Winfrey, and Harland David Sanders—aka Colonel Sanders of KFC fame—all made it. They turned their disappointments into unimaginable success. The same can be said of many famous Jamaicans you see today who failed at business and academic pursuits but never threw in the towel.

Have you suffered failure or setbacks? Has your marriage has gone bad? Have you lost your job? Has your business crashed? Has your visa has been revoked, and all that is staring you in the face is starting over? Well, there is hope. There is absolutely nothing wrong with starting over, turning over a new page. Hope doesn't have an expiry date and it springs eternal. Again the old adage reminds us: if you can look up, you can get up and start again.

> And we know that all things work together for the good of them that love God, to them who are the called according to His purpose. (Romans 8:28)

For the LORD thy God will hold thy right hand

saying unto thee, Fear not; I will help thee.

(Isaiah 41:13)

Natural pregnancies last for approximately nine months. However, when you are pregnant with purpose, dreams, and aspirations, it will take you much more time to give birth. Sometimes it will take up to ten to fifteen years or even longer before the delivery can come forth thus making manifest the gift that God has blessed you with. For some persons, giving birth to purpose may take a shorter time. Nevertheless, what is important is giving birth to your dreams. Interestingly, as you give birth, there may be incremental growth along the road to your success and purpose. No matter how small the growth is, celebrate, throw a party. The big delivery is coming soon.

Get Ready to Push

Like a woman who may have excruciating pains before delivery, you may well have to go through your pains before birth. She wants to see the bundle of joy, and she follows the doctor's or midwife's instructions all through the period of pushing. The same may well be true of you. When your pain comes, it may come in the form of frustration, disappointments, mistrust, disloyalty, and a lack of funds. These are pains of distractions as throbbing as they may be.

Your pain may seem long, but joy is coming. When these obstacles present themselves, get into the push position mentally, and push until you overcome. Push until you are successful and accomplish your dreams. In this push position, you can curse all you want, but you can never give up on yourself or your dreams of becoming who you are called to become. You exist for a purpose. Purpose protects you from intimidation. If you know your purpose in life, no one can question why you are living. Furthermore, no one can frighten a person who knows why he or she is living. Do understand that purpose cannot be derailed or aborted. Purpose is God-driven, and God will not allow you to abort your purpose.

It matters not where you were born; you are pregnant with the power to achieve, succeed, and excel. Let no one take that power from you or tell you your pregnancy is a phantom. Prove to your cynics, skeptics, and doubters that if greatness can come out of Nazareth, then you will give birth to promise and dreams. Whatever your dreams are, they cannot be too big.

Do not build your house on the street called Ordinary; it's far better to take up residence on Extraordinary Boulevard. Extraordinary people have jumbo-sized dreams and visions that most persons can visualize. Be like Sarah and Abraham of the Bible who both had a son (Isaac) and all this happened when they were preparing to go to the grave, not to bed. It was a ridiculous blessing from God. God ended up making Sarah laugh: "God has made me laugh, and all who hear will laugh with me" (Genesis 21:6 NKJV). So why do you think God can't do the same for you? I encourage you to step out and take it by genuine force.

When you feel the pain of your figurative pregnancy, laugh your way into your purpose, into your success, and to the top of your game. God has a ridiculous blessing for you. Overcome your pain with faith and trust and confidence in God.

Overcome the notion that you must be regular ... it robs
you of the chance to be extraordinary. – Uta Hagen

Is anything too hard for the LORD?-(Genesis 18:14)

Prayer

Majestic God and Father of heaven and earth, today I come before Thee asking You to teach me never to absorb or accept failure as final, but to see the lessons that can be learnt. Help me, Lord, to mount up with wings like an eagle, to run and not be weary and walk and not faint. Amen.

CHAPTER 3

Fear Is a Spirit

Fear is, I believe, a most effective tool in destroying the soul of an individual and the soul of people. – **Anwar Sadat**

According to Wikipedia, fear is an emotion induced by perceived danger or threat, which causes physiological changes and ultimately behavioral changes.

Fear will tell a person, "You cannot make it. You cannot accomplish such heights. You will never come out of this situation. You will never give birth to your dreams and aspirations."

You must not at any time give in to fear. Theologically, fear is a spirit. It will paralyze or cripple your gifts, dreams, success, activities, and thought processes. Fear is a prison. If you allow it to take you over, it will imprison you and everything that you desire to achieve.

Fear is all around us. We feel it coming through the TV, social media, the radio, everywhere, yet you must not fall prey to it. In many cases steel bars surround our homes with high-tech alarm systems attached. Fear has led to all of this. If you ever allow yourself to be locked into a box because of the spirit of fear, your mind will be captured and captivated by it; hence you become a captive of fear. That's why the Bible is clear on this matter: "God hath not given us the spirit of fear; but of power, and of love, and of a sound mind" (2 Timothy 1:7).

The Power of Fear

We are people with innate power, and we should use this dynamite power to conquer and overcome obstacles that are placed in our path. When fear and terror are allowed to take over our lives, we hand over power to another spirit, and that spirit will control our minds like a puppet on a string. It was the journalist Soledad O'Brien who intimates that "I've learned that fear limits you and your vision. It serves as blinders to what may be just a few steps down the road for you. The journey is valuable, but believing in your talents, your abilities, and your self-worth can empower you to walk down an even brighter path. Transforming fear into freedom—how great is that?"

How many times have we allowed the whole matter of fear to stop us dead in our tracks? The fear of the unknown more often than not, halts our progress in life. So frequently we find ourselves in a box called fear, terror, or trepidation, not wanting to launch out into something bigger and better.

Fear dries up our self-confidence and our ability to achieve great exploits. And so I love Marcus Garvey's understanding of confidence. He said, "If you have no confidence in self, you are twice defeated in the race of life." He further

> So frequently we find ourselves in a box called fear, terror, or trepidation, not wanting to launch out into something bigger and better.

stated that "with confidence, you have won before you have started." It suggests therefore that confidence, trust, and belief in oneself are important attributes to be cultivated when pursuing set goals.

Our minds should never be ruled by fear, anxiety or worry. If you believe that you were created for a desired purpose, you will fulfill the purpose for which you were created by God. Fear, depression, and paranoia should not crowd or take over your thoughts.

The opposite of fear is faith. Faith, according to Paul in Hebrews 11:1, "is the substance of things hoped for, the evidence of the things not seen." Faith in God removes all fears. It causes us to have an abiding confidence, hope, and trust in God. Therefore, you cannot rest your faith in God and at the same time harbor fear of failure. The two are like oil and water: they just don't mix.

Faith then is allowing you to reach for the unseen, but this faith must be laced with prayer and preparation. The groundwork must be established. You cannot hope for a job at an established business organization or want to attend university without making the necessary preparations. According to James 2:26, "Faith without works is dead"—dead as dirt. This means you must make preparation in order to activate your faith, and when you do so, fear should be neutralized.

Fear can be likened to a prison. Therefore, do not allow it to imprison your thoughts. That's why you are given a sound mind by God. So activate your faith as you launch out but prepare the ground first, so when the seeds of greatness are planted, the rewards will be inordinate.

You gain strength, courage, and confidence by every experience in which you really stop to look fear in the face. You are able to say to yourself, 'I lived through this horror. I can take the next thing that comes along. – Eleanor Roosevelt

But without faith it is impossible to please him: for he that cometh to God must believe that

he is, and that he is a rewarder of them that diligently seek him. (Hebrews 11:6)

Prayer

Great and mighty God of Zion, heaven and earth are full of Your glory. In this hour I call on You to examine my heart and remove all fears. I know fear is not of You but of the old adversary, whose job is to steal, kill, and destroy. Give me now the strength to walk in faith, hope, and love and not in fear. Amen.

CHAPTER 4

Stop Being a Parked Car

Do not go where the path may lead, go instead

where there is no path and leave a trail.

– Ralph Waldo Emerson

In this world many cars are parked and not going anywhere. They have been parked so long, they have started to rust, rot and disintegrate. They are basically ready for the scrap heap.

Many young people today who are purpose-driven and blessed with good parents or guardians oftentimes find themselves with friends and acquaintances who can be considered parked cars. While we are not consigning these associates to the scrap heap, these are people who are not going anywhere. Most times their view on life is totally different and upside down. These individuals who fall in the parked car category have a view of life that is simply pedestal, and the world owes them something. They get up each day without purpose or dreams.

Well, it's time to shed or divorce yourselves from such friends—yes, your "parrie," "benchie," or "dawg." The fact of life is, if you cannot pull these persons up to your standard, it's time to let them go. It's time for you to fly out of that nest. Get off that road. If you fail to annul the relationship, the parked car will make you stationary; you can't move. In other words, their standards will become yours eventually. Don't settle for rust and then dust; that's what you get from a car that is parked for far too long. Wake up, surge forward, and do something positive with your life, today.

The Whitney Houston song "One Moment in Time" (official video) gives us a clear picture that there is no way one can reach one's summit while running with the wrong people.

Soaring above the Cloud and the Crowd

The suggestion therefore is, do an evaluation of your friends, because who you run with many times determines where you are going. Today's young people must take on an *eagle mentality* and so soar above the clouds of life and the crowd as well. Eagles are symbols of honor, determination, bravery, beauty, pride, grace, and strength.

Eagles are special creatures and are blessed with several characteristics that are worth being adopted by humans. One is that they flock together. These birds fly with their kind only, most times ten thousand feet in altitude. If they are seen with other creatures, it is to seek something to eat. There is a popular idiom that many of us grew up on: "birds of a feather flock together." This is true of the eagle and many of us humans. Evidently, eagles don't run with ground doves, grass quits, pigeons, or common fowls (chicken); they fly with their kind.

Young people should be encouraged to get out of the lane where there is negative energy and the ultimate pessimists. Fly with those who hold a positive outlook and thinking. Run with those with whom you can depend on to elevate and develop your thoughts.

To be your better self, you need to leave the "common fowl" state of mind behind and soar like eagles. Most times we are the ones who stop ourselves from progressing because of the friends with whom we run or are associated. As was outlined in chapter 3, God has a ridiculous blessing for you. However, those you travel with can detain or derail your blessings, thus causing your gift to be stifled or stymied. Choose your friends wisely. You may well have to handpick those to come with you to Mount Moriah. Some persons may well have to stay with the asses.

> God has a ridiculous blessing for you.

Your Gift Will Open Doors

It is your gift that will help move you through life. It is your gift that will make you earn and provide for your family. It is your gift that will cause you to affect and impact human development in a positive way.

> A man's gift maketh room for him, and bringeth
>
> him before great men. (Proverbs 18:16)

So, when you choose to park, be careful with whom you park. Abram in Genesis 12:1–4 was told by God to leave his family and his father's house and go to a land that He would show him. If you are to get to where you want to, most times you have to leave some of your favorite people behind. Please don't be sorry about it. Like a deciduous tree that sheds its leaves annually, you have to learn to do the same. Detach yourself from people who have become baggage and who are holding you back with their negative lips and thoughts. If such persons cannot be pulled up to your expectations and standards, it's time to do some shedding.

One other unique feature of the eagle is that when it gets old and its feathers are worn and slowing it down, the bird will literally retire in the rocks to pluck off the old feathers and beat its beak on the rock to remove it. Again, there may be some friends who for one reason or the other are holding you back. In a nice, diplomatic manner, you need to shed them like the eagle removes those feathers.

Natural ability is important, but you can go far without it if you have the focus, drive, desire and positive attitude. – Kirsten Sweetland

And we know that for those who love God all things work together for good, for those who are called according to his purpose. (Romans 8:28 ESV)

Prayer

Heavenly lover and father of hope, grace, and peace, in the mighty name of Jesus Christ I salute and adore You. Today let me know Your will for my life. Teach me, gracious God, never to lose sight of where You are directing me. Communicate to me also to be the best of me, so I can use my gifts of time, talent, and treasure to worship You. Amen.

CHAPTER 5

Ingratitude Is a Sin

A grateful heart is a beginning of greatness. It is an expression of humility. It is a foundation for the development of such virtues as prayer, faith, courage, contentment, happiness, love, and well-being. – James E. Faust

Being grateful is an attitude and an attribute that all should seek to adopt especially in today's world. I find that in today's fast-paced world, many of us are not so thankful or grateful to those who have helped us along the way. Many people find it very challenging to praise or commend the other person or just to give kudos when required. In other words, we are not quick to praise or elevate, yet we are super quick to condemn. We are not swift to say, "Thank you, your assistance was tremendous," or even to say to another human being, "You look good today, radiant, handsome, or beautiful." Many find such phrases difficult to utter.

These are the little things that help to build character. These soft skills are gradually disappearing from us, and we wonder why so many of us are coarse and uncouth.

Ingratitude can be regarded as a sin. Numerous people have thrown stones behind them upon reaching a place of comfort and luxury. Such people fail to remember where they are coming from or who helped them along the way. The challenge then is never to allow ingratitude to cloud your path, thinking, and judgment.

Gratitude versus Ingratitude

There is a story in Luke 17 of ten lepers who suffered from a particular incurable disease, no doubt for years. These were society's outcasts, rejects. They were rejected by their families, friends, and communities. However, their situation changed when, through their loud cries, they got the attention of Jesus the Christ. In the end all ten were healed of the dreaded disease of leprosy.

Several themes can be taken from the story. Nevertheless, the one that is most suited for the present context is that of gratitude. The story is simple, yet profound. The Bible is clear: only one of the ten lepers returned to express thanks and to show his gratefulness. The other nine were never appreciative for their transformation and saw no need to return with grateful hearts. In verses 17–18 of the said text, Jesus asked, "Were there not ten cleansed? But where are the nine? Were there not any found who returned to give glory to God except this foreigner?"

Biblically, God values service of praise and thanksgiving. We ought to be thankful to God for everything, be it great or small. Our lives, gifts, and accomplishments belong to God, loaned to us. Never forget then to praise and honor God for these wonders.

As humans, it is expected of us to place value on gratitude. We should never find ourselves at a place similar to that of the nine lepers who did not return to express their appreciation.

There are endless examples today. I have seen parents, especially single mothers and fathers (yes, fathers too!), who gave up everything, placing their lives on hold to give their children the very best opportunities. However, when the dust is settled at the end of the day, what the giver receives would cause your stomach to churn.

There are many mothers who have scrubbed floors, washed people's dirty clothes, and walked the streets in the hot sun selling or vending to make ends meet. Yet when they are up in age, their children who can help are too busy doing everything except helping them.

No matter the circumstance, we should be grateful and be indebted to those who cared, motivated, and inspired us

> No matter the circumstance, we should be grateful and be indebted to those who cared, motivated, and inspired us along life's pathway.

along life's pathway. Someone once said God hates ugly, and make no mistake, this is one ugly attitude, which I cannot doubt that God abhors.

Please don't be like the Christian man who prayed fervently for a motorbike so that he could get to church on time and do all the things he wanted to do for God. Of course, he got a motorbike, a powerful one too. Rather than continue attending church to give God thanks and praise for the gift, he used it for the purpose of selling ice cream and other frozen novelties, driving pass the church shouting, "Fudgy or creamy," and blowing his "creamy horn" while passing.

Again, God values the service of thanksgiving and praise both to Him and to those around us. The encouragement is, never forget those who helped you along the way and learn also to pay it forward or reciprocate. When was the last time you called someone who helped to shape your life and future?

Our hearts are built to give and be grateful. So why
cause the heart to flounder from unthankfulness. When
we love, truly love, we give of ourselves, time and gifts
without measure. When we love we hold nothing

> *back ... so praise and thanksgiving becomes a natural*
>
> *part of our human experience.* —Unknown

Go right ahead and show unequivocally that spirit of gratitude and appreciation to those who have helped to guide you along the road of success. Don't be afraid to show those who have cared for you, wiped your nose, and changed your diaper your avid appreciation. The sin of ingratitude is worse than witchcraft. Yes! That's how terrible being ungrateful really is.

Demonstrate that you are really grateful for the opportunity your parents gave you by bringing you into this world. Your mommy did not abort you. Your childhood may not have been the best, but look at you now. You may have nothing tangible to give, but just sharing quality time of fellowship could make a world of difference. Good fellowship can breathe happiness and contentment, something money can't necessarily buy.

Gratitude is not only the greatest of virtues,

but the parent of all the others.

–Marcus Tullius Cicero

We learned about gratitude and humility—that so many people had a hand in our success, from the teachers who inspired us to the janitors who kept our school clean … and we were taught to value everyone's contribution and treat everyone with respect. –Michelle Obama

Finally, brethren, whatsoever things are true, whatsoever things are honest, whatsoever things are just, whatsoever things are pure, whatsoever things are lovely, whatsoever things are of good report; if there be any virtue, and if there be any praise, think on these things. –(Philippians 4:8)

Prayer

Dear Lord, Shepherd and Savior, I come humbly before You to thank You for all Your goodness toward me and my family. In this sweet hour of prayer, I ask You kindly to teach me how to love and appreciate You more. Remove from me the spirit of ingratitude, and open the doors of thanksgiving and appreciation for those who helped me along the way. Amen.

Chapter 6

Expecting a Return on the Investment

An investment in knowledge pays the best

interest. –Benjamin Franklin

As humans it's natural to expect and want the best for our children, and I mean if we really care and love them. To get the best from our children we must invest in their lives from as early as in the womb. We have to invest time as well as human and financial resources. What a mother feeds her child's mind and stomach with, can have a direct effect on the psychological and mental growth of that child.

Though their children are not "objects," parents must seek to invest in their children's well-being, which is their academic, physical, social, mental, and spiritual growth.

Far too many of our children are living without the right investors. And we wonder why they are not giving us any returns. It's time we invest more in the lives of our children if we want better communities and societies.

An investment in your children is an investment in the future. Your children should know that an investment requires a return as part of the end game. When one invests in stocks or bonds, the returns may be variable, but one is likely to earn. The truth is, there is always an expectation of the return. The same is true for your children. Ecclesiastes 11:1 (KJV) puts it this way: "Cast thy bread upon the waters, for thou shall find it after many days." When you invest your time and resources and create the right atmosphere for growth, development, and success, it should not be business as usual as it relates to your expectations and returns on that investment. A return is expected at the end of the day, even if it comes late.

As outlined previously, who your children run with may derail or crash the investment. It simply means, as far as possible, without apology, you should know with whom your children are socializing. Why? If your children are of any value to you, it's important that you pay keen attention. Do not wait until things have fallen apart before you act. Look for the signs such as coming home late regularly, change in the color of the lips, using the cell phone at odd hours of the night, behavioral changes, and so many others. Delay is perceived as being dangerous. Act when you see things not lining up with your expectations.

Counting the Cost

Supporting a child financially, socially, and otherwise through primary and secondary schools is a serious investment. When one looks at how much is invested in bus fare and lunch each month alone, it is quite a big investment, not to mention the multiplier effect over many years of schooling at the levels. So if you were to literally do monthly and yearly calculations, it might blow your mind. The cost must be calculated and counted. There is a cost to everything, be it biblical, psychological, social, or financial. Didn't Jesus pay it all on the cross? So there is a cost for what you have been doing and continue to do for your children.

Many parents who are seeking the best for their children are selling in the streets, performing domestic duties, and doing God knows what to give their children the very best. The point we are trying to raise is that no matter where you are in the world, you can identify with how much sacrifice, financially and otherwise, you will make for your children to get a sound education. Investing in your children should never be a jocular affair. The calculation that may be done many times does not include:

- Additional books
- Extra lessons
- Field trips
- Examination fees (where required)
- And many other things throughout the child's school life

Be reminded that inflation can be a spanner in the financial gearbox. From this basic calculation, you parents can see how much you are investing in your children's future. Why then are you leaving your investment to be eaten by social vultures and ambushers of dreams?

So a word to the wise is sufficient. Parents/investors, here are a few tips:

- Plan carefully and wisely for your children.
- Keep in touch with your children.
- Build a solid relationship with your children.
- Be your children's coach, not necessarily their friend.
- In the "stands of life", be that one spectator who will be always cheering your children.
- Be your children's motivator, commander, and encourager.
- Support your children's dreams and ambitions.
- Never give up on your children (failure is never final).
- Have an awareness of your children's friends.
- Do not discourage them, urge them on.

- Never be afraid to add to the investment once the returns are good.

So as you invest, place more attention on your children than on the price of the cell phone that you give them. Many times, the schoolbag of your children, in whom you have invested so much, is empty, yet the cell phone is valued at $30,000 (US$200) or more.

If you are a teenager or a young adult reading this book, your parents require of

> Procrastination is the thief of time. Do not allow it to steal your dreams.

you a return on their investment of time, talent, and treasure. Many parents have suffered shame and abuse, yet they came through for their children. Procrastination is the thief of time. Do not allow it to steal your dreams. Focus on the set target, never deflecting. Always looking at the prize ahead.

As you invest, keep reminding your children never to settle for second best or mediocrity. Fairly and squarely, they are going to take what belongs to them.

Parents should understand they are major partners in the business called family. You help to socially, morally, ethically, and spiritually shape the development of your children. As a parent, you are a social engineer affecting, impacting, and influencing the future. Since you are a partner, participate. Do not be a spectator, leaving it all on the teacher or someone else. A partner who holds shares in a business is not likely to stand and watch the business shrink and lapse. Apply the same to your children's future development.

Invest in Self as Well

Whereas it is necessary and important to invest in your children, don't forget to invest in yourselves. Find some time to pay attention to your:

- Health
- Education
- Relationship
- Goals (you can't forget your vision board)

Never believe that you can be duplicated. We have been given one body for a season. Choose to do what is right and good with it. It is the temple of God and should be protected.

Lo, children are an heritage of the Lord: and the fruit of the womb is his reward. (Psalm 127:3)

We have an obligation and a responsibility to be investing in our students and our schools. We must make sure that people who have the grades, the desire and the will, but not the money, can still get the best education possible. –Barack Obama

Give, and it shall be given unto you; good measure, press down, and shaken together, and running over, shall men give into your bosom. For with the same measure that ye mete withal it shall be measured to you again. (Luke 6:38)

Prayer

Loving God, in the name of Jesus Christ, teach me to always love and appreciate. Cheer me on when I am low and demotivated. Give me the strength and support to believe in myself as well as the desire to look for good in all persons. Help me, Lord, to be an encourager and a motivator. Amen.

CHAPTER 7

The True Bread that Satisfies

I believe many of us are over nourished on

entertainment junk food and undernourished

on the bread of life. –Dallin H. Oaks

And as they were eating, Jesus took bread, and blessed it, and brake it, and gave it to the disciples, and said, Take, eat; this is my body. And he took the cup, and gave thanks, and gave it to them, saying, Drink ye all of it; For this is my blood of the new testament, which is shed for many for the remission of sins. (Matthew 26:26–28)

So many people seek satisfaction in the wrong places for the hunger and the thirst that they bear. God has created all humans with the capacity to hunger and thirst after something more than the usual fish and bread, along with the temporal things of this life. God, the great designer, has built us with a God-sized appetite for more. It is for more of Him and not for more of our fallen world.

Human Responsibility

The human's responsibility is to seek the only source that can satisfy this hunger or longing. It must be noted that, because there is a lack of knowledge and understanding—or an ignorance of what this hunger or craving is, where it originated, and where the true solution and satisfaction lies—many people go about seeking for satisfaction and fulfillment in the wrong places.

There is an old saying that "one cannot put a square peg in a round hole." There is nothing in this world that can satisfy the deepest need and hunger of the fallen soul but the *true Bread of Life, Jesus Christ,* the Son of God.

Looking back over the passage of time, from the days when Israel came out of Egypt's bondage to our present day, the true Bread of Life was always better than the manna in the wilderness. The true Bread of Life was always better than the quails that fell in their camp. The true Bread of Life was better than the water from the bitter Marah. The true Bread of Life was far better than the corn that they enjoyed in Canaan. Friends, although those foods were suitable for the time, they never truly satisfied Israel's hungry and lustful souls. The Israel of old was still hungry and miserable in their souls.

In the New Testament Jesus chided or rebuked His followers, telling them that they were seeking Him not for the word of God but for the fish and bread: "Verily, verily, I say unto you, Ye seek me, not because ye saw the miracles, but because ye did eat of the loaves, and were filled" (John 6:26).

Jesus Christ continued His warning to His followers in no uncertain terms. He warned them: "Labour not for the meat which perisheth, but for that meat which endureth unto everlasting life, which the Son of man shall give unto you: for him hath God the Father sealed" (John 6:27). Today that same hunger exists and is prevalent in every nation under heaven. The tragedy is that the more man gets what he wants, it is the less he wants what he gets. Wrong priorities and wrong solutions. Jesus alone is the true Bread of Life that satisfies all hungry lives.

Never Forget the True Bread of Life

Without fear of contradiction, there is no bread like the true Bread of Life, Jesus Christ. So while we seek to maximize our time on earth and achieve all there is, we should never be satisfied with the two slices of the bread only. The encouragement, therefore, is never to forget the true Bread of Life in your pursuit of your dreams and aspirations. He came down from heaven to satisfy your spiritual hunger.

The message to our world, today as always—with its

> Without fear of contradiction, there is no bread like the true Bread of Life, Jesus Christ.

wars and its wrongdoings, with its toils and its troubles, its cares and its complexities, its weapons of mass destruction and its wanton waste of lives, its fears and its failures—is that there has never been anything else as suitable as the Lord Jesus, the Bread of Life. Jesus is all the bread that you need while you are on your way to heaven. In this temporal world you are challenged not to settle for two slices of the bread, and so you are being encouraged to do the same as it relates to Jesus Christ, the Bread of Life.

The entire loaf is available to you. He is accessible in full. Will you have the whole loaf as you strive toward your goals? Nothing is odd with reaching for the stars and at the same time having the Bread of Life in a sincere and committed way journeying with you. This will be joy unspeakable and full of glory.

This chapter wraps up with a profound recommendation: Try the way, eat of the Bread of Life, trust the Lord Jesus Christ. One of the objectives of this book is to tell you, with every fervor and faith, to taste and see that the Lord is good. You can know this bread that came down from heaven and how satisfying, how suitable, and how sweet He is. Trust Him.

And Jesus said unto them, I am the bread of life: he that cometh to me shall never hunger; and he that believeth on me shall never thirst. (John 6:35)

Prayer

Eternal God and Father, You who stretch forth the sky like a curtain, in Your Son's name I come. Help me to understand who You are and what You want of me. As I seek to go after my goals and dreams, teach me, Lord, to accept You in my heart as the Bread of Life. Amen.

Chapter 8

It's Time to Step Out of Your Prison

When you are imprisoned, you can't enjoy the
benefits of being alive. You can't educate yourself and
discover the beauty of the world. –Lily Amis

There are many persons across the world who are in prison. They are incarcerated for one reason or another. In America, for example, there are more black persons who are in prison than their white counterparts. When you are imprisoned in the physical sense, your freedom is taken away and opportunities are removed.

Many will die in these state and government facilities. Some will never see the light of freedom again.

For those who are locked away, freedom starts in the mind. It starts with understanding who you are and why you were created by God, not to be locked in a mental prison but to be freed.

However, there are many who are walking around free from the bars of a physical prison, but mentally they are in prison and fighting to be released. These persons are locked away in a mental penitentiary, and they are aggressively fighting to get out. Like many of those in the physical prison, many walking around with a smile will die in their mental penitentiary if they are not freed.

The Screams

Interestingly, there are so many persons, young and old alike walking around yet locked away in a mental jail. This is a prison, where many of us are the contractors, constructing our own self-penitentiary. For those who are locked away, freedom starts in the mind. It starts with understanding who you are and why you were created by God, not to be locked in a mental prison but to be freed.

God did not create us to be locked away in self-isolation and a mental prison. You dress well, speak well, smell fresh, and look good, yet you are fighting day and night to get out of your prison. Some days you're screaming, yet no one is hearing you. Well, it's time to take the first step, so that God can step in.

Do you know that you are a member of God's chosen generation? The word of God declares in 1 Peter 2:9 (emphasis added), "But ye are a *chosen generation*, a royal priesthood, a holy nation, a peculiar people; that ye should shew forth the praises of him who hath called you out of darkness into his marvellous light." Question, do you believe that you are chosen, selected by God? If you do, you need to stop making decisions and leaving God out.

Part of the reason why many are in a mental prison could well be the result of psychological conflicts. Do you know that God wants the best for all of us? And despite your circumstance and situation He still has you on His mind and wants to see you blossom and shine like the morning star? Jeremiah 29:11 declares that "I know the thoughts that I think towards you saith the LORD, thoughts of peace and not of evil, to give you an expected end." This verse of scripture does not mean we will be spared suffering, pain, hardship, setbacks, or dejections, but the God of heaven and earth will see us through to a glorious conclusion.

God's Agenda

Our brothers and sisters, God has an agenda for you—an agenda for good that is full of hope. Additionally, God's desire is to use you for good. But first He needs to release you from your mental prison and give you inner peace, the peace that surpasses all understanding.

The simple principle is that Jesus Christ went to the cross centuries ago, to free all of us from all fears and mental penitentiaries in which we may find ourselves. Interestingly, many who go to church daily or weekly are shut away in a mental jail. Freedom is here in the form of Jesus Christ. Isaiah 61:1 states that "the Spirit of the Lord GOD is upon me;

because the LORD hath anointed me to preach good tidings unto the meek; he hath sent me to bind up the brokenhearted, to proclaim liberty to captives and the opening of the prison to them that are bound." You need to make the first move and allow God to do the rest.

So, if you are tangled up and feel incapacitated in your mind, because of the burdens of your life, Jesus's love can free you of that burden. The freedom from your prison starts in your mind and your taking that initial step. If you are not freed of the encumbrances of this life, you will always feel as if you are drowning and sinking to the bottom of life's pit.

A mind that is locked away in a mental prison cannot live and enjoy the beauty of what life has to offer through Jesus Christ. A life tormented by living in a mental prison will lead to you walking around sad and dejected. A life lived in a mental penitentiary is likely to cause you to lose out on the opportunities and the blessings God has in store for you.

Second Best

Do understand that sometimes you are in a mental penitentiary, tormented by the behavior of your spouse, a friend, or a relative. Sometimes your place of work is your prison, and you find yourself locked in. For many, their relationships are abusive, devoid of love and companionship and the whole nine yards.

Perhaps you find yourself in a prison hoping one day to be freed. At the same time your happiness, joy, and peace are all gone or going. You have even lost your dance. If so, it's time to start looking to God. Believing in who you are and why you are on the earth. You are here never to be second best or to be trapped by circumstance, situation, status quo, or anyone else's thoughts or feelings.

To help free yourself from your mental prison, choose to

- ***Change how your heart feels and allow Jesus to lead.*** David in Psalm 51:11–12 pleaded with God to create in him a clean heart, and renew a right spirit in him.

He further asked God to restore unto him the joy of His salvation. David was messed up big-time. He had gone to bed with Bathsheba, thus committing adultery, and murdered her husband Uriah to cover it up. His mind was in confusion and a big muddle, so he cried out to God for a changed heart. You can do the same.

Your mental prison may have caused you to be in a circle of confusion, and the life you were expecting is falling apart due to your behavior and the decisions you've taken. God is waiting on you to cry out to Him as David did. A changed heart gives you access to bountiful blessings. Understand that challenges are part of the process of getting to the mountaintop. However, God in Jesus Christ will, in the end, give you beauty for ashes. Are you ready to make the bold move towards giving your heart to Jesus?

- **Change your outlook**

  To escape from your mental prison, you must change how you see yourself. You cannot be looking at yourself the same way every day and expect to be different. Find Jesus Christ, the chief Liberator. He is available for all who find themselves spiritually and mentally oppressed.

  Paul and Silas were in a physical prison in Acts chapter 16, and while being there, they started a praise party, and the doors of the jail were released. Jesus Christ can do the same for you. He can release you from your mental penitentiary so that you come out singing, praising, and dancing. God is waiting on you to liberate you. Are you ready to step forward and allow Him to?

- **Change your focus**

  The woman in Mark chapter 5 with the issue of blood suffered for twelve long years. During that time, she visited many doctors. Her financial resources were depleted, and rather than getting better, she got worse. She got out of her situation when she changed her focus to Jesus Christ who was coming her way. The woman shook off the critics and the naysayers, lifted her faith, and made a move in right direction—a move that led her to touch the hem of Jesus's garment. Are you ready to make that step to come out of your mental prison? To shift your focus to Jesus Christ, and watch yourself grow exponentially in all areas of your life?

- *Change your thought process*

  If you want to move out of that house called a mental prison, you have to change your thought process—that is, how you process things mentally, whether negatively or positively. Burdens should be left at Jesus's feet. But first, you must make the necessary provision. God moves when you move. God acts when you act. Positive spirits attract positive people.

- **Change how you see yourself**

  It was the psalmist David who said, "I am fearfully and wonderfully made." Simply put, he is taking the image of God, living out Genesis 1:27: "So God created man in His own image; in the image of God, he created him; male and female He created them." If this is so, why are you walking around like you are nobody, as if you are no good and of no value? That attitude needs major adjustment. You are who you think you are. Since God has made you in His own image, stop looking or waiting for people to validate you.

- **Change your circle of friends**

  Many times, we find ourselves stuck in a mental penitentiary merely because of the friends we have in our circle. These friends may not be helping us in any way, shape, or form to escape the torture of the prison.

  In that case, what do you do? Learn to sift. Be selective about whom you allow in your inner circle. This may be difficult, but it must be done. The method of sifting may allow you to break out of your mental prison. Like what happened in Acts 5: 17–21 with Peter and the apostles, God may just be getting ready to send an angel to release you from that mental prison. But are you ready to make the move? Are you willing to stand and say to yourself, "Enough is enough"? Will you say, "I have had enough"? Get this: there comes a time when you have to talk to yourself. Encourage and motivate yourself.

There is a north for all of us. When you are doing well in all areas of your career, you should be heading north. On the contrary, if things are not going well, life may well be heading south. You can determine which direction you want your life to go. Have you forgiven yourself yet for all those poor decisions you have made over these many years? Forgiveness will help to liberate you from your imprisoned mind.

Forgiveness is for yourself because it frees you. It

lets you out of that prison you put yourself in.

–Louise L. Hay

A mind that dwells in the past builds a prison it cannot

escape. Control your mind, or it will control you, and you

will never break through the walls it builds. –A. G. Riddle

Stand fast therefore in the liberty wherein Christ

hath made us free, and be not entangled again

with the yoke of bondage. (Galatians 5:1)

Prayer

Eternal God and Father, in the name of Jesus Christ, I pray for strength and for Your peace that surpasses all understanding. Come now, heavenly Father, through your Holy Spirit, and free me from the bondage of sin and unforgiveness. Take up residence in my heart forevermore, I pray. I receive Your salvation now in Jesus's name. Amen.

Lightning Source UK Ltd.
Milton Keynes UK
UKHW041301131121
393906UK00002B/89